Advent

*A Spiritual Walk
Toward Christmas*

Chip Bristol

&

Kelly Rightsell

All profits from this book go to Crayons Matter, a not-for-profit whose mission is to inspire children to uncover their potential and purpose through creative art by providing much-needed backpacks filled with school supplies to children around the world. Learn more: https://crayonsmatter.org

We want to offer a special note of thanks to Richelle Thompson and her team at Crown Publishing for their invaluable feedback, enormous creativity, and hard work. This book would not have been possible without their help.

Scripture quotations are from the New Revised Standard Version of the Bible, copyright ©1989 the National Council of the Churches of Christ in the United States of America.

Psalm quotations are from the Book of Common Prayer.

ISBN: 9798343192087

Advent

A Spiritual Walk Toward Christmas

Chip Bristol

&

Kelly Rightsell

Crown Publishing

Fort Thomas, Kentucky

We dedicate this book to our parents,
the ones who first introduced us
to the wonder of Advent
and blessing of Christmas.
CB and KR

Note: There is a Spotify mix (by Chip Bristol) entitled "Advent" with 25 pieces to complement the meditations in this book.

Contents

ALMIGHTY GOD, you have given us the
season of Advent to prepare a space
in our hearts for the coming of your son.
O Come, O come, Emmanuel,
God be with us as we join the angels and
archangels, as we walk with Mary and Joseph,
and as we sit beside the shepherds and kings
to behold the wonder of your grace.
All of this we pray in the name of your son,
the Word made flesh, Jesus the Christ. *Amen*.

Anticipation

The angel said to her, "Do not be afraid, Mary, for you have found favor with God. And now, you will conceive in your womb and bear a son, and you shall name him Jesus.—LUKE 1:30-31

The voicemail was unmistakable: my eldest sister called to inform me a package was on its way. She had gone through my recently deceased mother's things and found the family creche. "You should have it," she said. "It'll be there in time for Advent."

I loved the creche as a child. I remember my mother bringing it up from the basement and unwrapping each piece. Now the creche was coming to my house. The thought awakened the child within me, and I needed to prepare a space.

The season of Advent is like that. It began when an unmistakable voice told a young woman she was going to bring God into the world. Those words echo across the centuries still. God is coming. God will be with us. Like many in Mary's day, the coming of the Messiah felt like a long-forgotten dream. Now, the time had come. She needed to prepare.

Anticipating God's arrival is what Advent is all about. The words spoken to Mary can be heard by the likes of you and me today. Sometimes, they come to us loud and clear. Other times, they come in a still, small voice. Regardless of how the words come, we're called to respond—and to get ready.

The Messiah is coming. May we all prepare a space to receive him.

For reflection

* What was December like in your childhood home?
* When you think of God being with us, what stirs within you?
* How will you prepare for God's coming this Advent?

Expectation

He will be great, and will be called the Son of the Most High, and the Lord God will give to him the throne of his ancestor David. He will reign over the house of Jacob forever, and of his kingdom there will be no end."
—Luke 1:32-33

The danger of anticipation is that it can quickly turn into expectation. The excitement of anticipating someone's arrival can quickly turn into expecting what that moment will be like. Whether it's a family vacation, a special dinner, or a long-awaited reunion with a loved one, our expectations paint a picture that often does not capture what eventually takes place. We picture what will happen and then resent the way things turn out.

"An expectation is a future resentment," someone wise once said, and it's particularly true when it comes to Christmas. Advent, the season of anticipation, often turns into a season of expectations, and by the time Christmas arrives, we feel let down or disappointed. Hearing beloved carols, seeing decorations, and gathering with loved ones are the season's gifts. As a child, I would shake with anticipation, which would often lead to expectations that were never realized. News of the creche's arrival from my mother's estate awakened that excitable child. I searched for the perfect place, picturing what it would look like and imagining my children would love it as much as I once did. I started having expectations.

The same was true 2,000 years ago. The Hebrew people had been promised a Messiah, and their anticipation turned to expectations over time. He would be a mighty warrior, said those who were resentful of Rome's occupation. He would be a great religious leader, said those who sought the relationship they once had with God. No wonder Jesus was such a surprise. Born to an unwed couple in a stable, Jesus and his birth were just the beginning of the countless ways he would surprise people.

Our desire for God runs deep, and we expect him to arrive in our lives in a particular way. God will come *this* way. *This* is what he will say and do. No wonder we are often disappointed with the way Christ comes into our lives. It might not be how we imagined, but the good news is that, while Jesus might not be what we expect, he's always more than we could hope for or imagine.

For reflection

⁎ Recall a time when your expectations spoiled a moment.
⁎ How might your expectations about God stand in your way this Christmas?
⁎ What would it be like to have unbridled anticipation with no expectations this Christmas?

Making Space

Then Mary said, "Here am I, the servant of the Lord; let it be to me according to your word." —LUKE 1:38

More than anything else, making space is what Advent is all about. During the year, let alone a lifetime, things accumulate. Our calendars fill, and concerns overflow. Entering the season of Advent, it's hard to imagine how to add one more thing to our lives. Just like I needed to clear a space for the creche, we all need to clear away some of the clutter and make room for what (or who) is coming.

Advent is about clearing, about making space. As the space around us gets cramped, we need to decide what matters at this sacred time of year. As the days grow shorter, we need to value each moment. As the days grow darker, we need to treasure the light.

We're better at adding than subtracting, but Advent asks us to take away the things that stand in the way of our welcoming God anew. Whether turning off the television or putting down the newspaper or phone, the ways to make space are endless. "You can't fill a glass that's already full," a friend once reminded me. So it is with our houses, our lives, and our souls.

Christmas is coming. Now is the time to prepare. The first step is making space.

For reflection

* What is something in your home you can remove if only during Advent?
* What is something you can take from your daily life to make more room?
* What is something that clutters your spiritual life and could be removed?

8

Memories

He has helped his servant Israel, in remembrance of his mercy, according to the promise he made to our ancestors, to Abraham and to his descendants forever. —LUKE 1:54-55

To make sense of the present, Mary looked to the past. There, she saw God's saving acts and believed she would now be a part of those saving acts in a new and profound way. So, too, when Advent comes, we often think of the past. Such memories shape the present.

When the creche arrived, I opened the package gingerly. Inside was the familiar red and green box with frayed edges. It was like holding a piece of my childhood in my hands. Leaning down, I thought I smelled my mother's perfume. Joy and sadness overwhelmed me at the same moment. The Christmas season can do that. Like no other time of year, the past and the present seem to walk side by side, and our senses bind them together.

Advent comes to us through the power of our senses, stirring them together into an emotional stew. The season awakens our souls through carols and sleighbells, food and candles, lights and decorations. There is no end to the sensory portals that bring us into the season and summon memories of seasons past. We walk hand in hand with our memories. It's an emotionally charged season, and we do well to proceed with caution.

For reflection

* What senses stir you the most at this time of year?
* What are your fondest memories? Do they also carry with them any sadness?
* How can you open this Christmas season like the gift it is?

Packaging

And she gave birth to her firstborn son and wrapped him in bands of cloth.
—LUKE 2:7A

It wasn't what I expected.

Instead of special wrapping, the familiar box was filled with crumpled pieces of newspaper wrapped around each figure. Like the box itself, the pieces looked weathered and smaller than I remembered. It was disappointing at first, but then I realized I needed to adjust my thinking. My memories had distorted, inflated, and romanticized things. Christmas often comes wrapped in ways we don't imagine.

As I picked up each piece and placed it on the counter, I thought about how I sometimes store God in a box. Boxes keep things safe. They also confine what's inside them. When something (or someone) is put in a box, it is easy to restrict or control what's inside. We do it with memories, people, and God.

As I unwrapped each figure of the creche, I thought about how God came as a baby, wrapped in swaddling clothes. He, too, was wrapped in ordinary "paper." It probably made no sense at the time; it may have even been a disappointment, but as we look back, the story makes all the sense in the world.

This is the season to open the boxes of our hearts and allow God to enter in whatever way he so chooses. He may arrive in ways smaller than we expect, wrapped in ways we couldn't have imagined, but what matters is that he comes. That, above all else, is the point.

May we recognize him and receive him once again.

For reflection

* What were your favorite Christmas decorations and traditions growing up?
* In what unexpected ways has Christmas come to you over the years?
* How can you open your heart this year and find the familiar, unexpected presence of God?

December 6

The Inn

There was no place for them in the inn. —LUKE 2:7

I remember it as if I were seven years old. A group of classmates were gathered at recess by the jungle gym, talking and laughing about something but refusing to let me join the group. It was my first memory of being excluded, but not the last. Each time it happens, I think about Mary and Joseph's arrival in Bethlehem and how it must have felt when they were turned away from the inn.

We live in a world where some people are "in" and others "out;" some are included, and others aren't. I suppose it's always been this way, but the child about to be born will have lots to say on the subject. In the stories he tells and the attention he gives, Jesus will cross the world's countless dividing lines. So much so it will cost him his life.

Inns come in all shapes and sizes, and it's only natural to want to be inside, close to where the action is, but from its beginning, the Christian story involves the crowd outside the inn. We can bemoan our being on the outside looking in, or we can look for the freedom of being outside—where Mary and Joseph were. Where Jesus was born.

For reflection

* Can you recall a moment when you were on the outside looking in?
* Did you accept it, or did you conform or try harder to get inside?
* How is God found outside the "inn," and what freedom is found outside?

The Door

He went to be registered with Mary, to whom he was engaged and who was expecting a child. —LUKE 2:5

The stable was the first piece I put in place. It was the biggest piece of the creche and framed the rest of the scene. While I looked at the stable, I couldn't help but think of the inn nearby and, more specifically, the door that was closed to Joseph and Mary. Because of the census, the inn was full. Joseph still knocked. It must have taken many attempts before the innkeeper heard them. He probably rolled his eyes. He'd already turned many away and was ready to do it again.

"Can I help you?" the innkeeper asked, peering around the edge of the thick door.

Joseph explained their situation and asked for lodging.

"Sorry, there's no room," the innkeeper said as he began to shut the door, only to notice the pregnant woman on the donkey. "There's a stable out back. You can sleep there," he offered before closing the door.

It's easy to judge the innkeeper, but the fact is we turn Jesus away all the time. God knocks, but we either pretend not to hear or make some excuse for not opening the door wide. "You've got the wrong person." "I'm really busy." "Another time, perhaps."

Advent is the season of knocking. It's the season to answer the door and invite Jesus in.

For reflection

* In what ways does a "door" stand between you and God?
* How has God knocked, and how have you turned him away?
* What would it look like for you to open the door and invite Jesus into your life?

19

The Stable

And while they were there, the time came for her to deliver her child.
—LUKE 2:6

When I think about the stable, I imagine the sound of Joseph and Mary's sandals on the dirt floor and see the straw strewn throughout. I can hear the animals in their stalls snorting and looking out at the intruders. Historians suggest the stable was more like a cave than a barn, but what is clear is that it was not a luxurious spot. The sounds from the crowd in the inn only accentuated the silence of the stable. Lit only by his lantern, Joseph searched frantically for a place for Mary to rest. The baby was coming.

How I wish I could have been there, over in a corner, crouched behind a bale of hay, watching Mary and Joseph look down at the newborn child. They wrapped the baby tightly in the clothes they could find and placed him in the feeding trough. At that moment, they were the first two to see the child. Somewhere within, they were the first to know the world would never be the same.

The stable is a vivid reminder that God usually enters the places out back, the places we hide, the places we'd like to forget. But it's often in such places God finds a home.

Lifting the stable of the creche into place, I gave thanks for such spaces, the places I hide but God finds, the quiet places with dim light. It's in such places that God's presence is always found.

For reflection

* Where is the stable in your life, the place out back you try to hide?
* Has God ever come into your life where or when you least expected?
* Why do you think God comes into our lives in such places?

December 9

The Animals

"The animals always come first," I remember announcing to my mother. I'm not sure why, but it became a tradition each year. One figure depicts a cow lying down; another one is standing. I always placed the cows on the right and put the sheep on the left.

I love that the Christmas story includes animals. It brings the story down to earth, so to speak, and reminds me that God is the God of *all creation*—you and me, and the animals, too. Animals are less complicated than we are. They live their lives and accept things as they are.

Placing the animals in the stable reminded me that we should follow their example. We should accept things as they are and stop trying to run the show. We should take our places and receive this gift of love given to all creation. Too often, I've tried to analyze what happened in the stable and debate the specifics with my theological arms crossed. I should be more like the animals and simply receive the gift.

When I was a boy, I had a funny-looking dog. He was grey with black spots. One day, our church invited us to bring our pets for a blessing. I couldn't wait. Even though my dog looked funny, beside the Golden Retrievers and Labradors, he was beautiful to me.

When I think about the stable with the animals gathered around the manger, I think back on that moment in church. God blesses *all* the animals, the purebreds and mutts alike.

It was the first of many times Jesus taught this most important lesson.

For reflection

★ What do you love most about animals?
★ What do the animals in the Christmas story have to teach us?
★ Do you believe God blesses purebreds and mutts alike?

The Donkey

Then there was the donkey!

I had always placed the donkey after the other animals and given him a place of honor. The cows and sheep just happened to be there. The donkey made it possible.

My father once wrote a Christmas carol about the donkey carrying Mary to Bethlehem. It always reminded me of the critical role the donkey played in the Christmas story. Because of him, they arrived in Joseph's ancestral home. "Good job," I can hear Joseph say as he unties the harness and gives his noble steed something to eat and drink.

The donkey makes me consider who the "donkeys" are in my life—the ones who might not appear all that special but who, in their own way, carry me safely and play an important role in my journey. Who do I dismiss who ends up making it possible for Christ to enter the world?

The Christmas story isn't something that only happened years ago. It continues to happen. Christ enters our world and becomes flesh on a daily basis if only we have eyes to see. Like the story long ago, it might happen in a place as simple as a stable, in the company of people as unimpressive as a group of mangy animals, and made possible because of a silly-looking donkey.

But Jesus comes and blessed be the ones who see it and are a part of it.

For reflection

* Do you know anyone who brings Christ into the world?
* Like the donkey, is it someone you'd least expect to play such a role?
* How might you follow the donkey's example and bring Christ into the world?

The Shepherds

And in that region there were shepherds living in the fields. —LUKE 2:8

I placed the shepherds beside the animals. For some reason, I've always had a thing for the shepherds. They were out in the field minding their own business, keeping watch over their flocks by night when an angel suddenly appeared. In typical fashion, they're told to fear not, but that's easier said than done. The shepherds were comfortable in the darkness, under the light of the moon and stars, where no one troubled them. All they had to do was take care of the sheep.

In the social food chain at the time, shepherds were low. There were many more important people in the world. Why would God choose shepherds of all people to be among the first to hear the good news of Christ's birth? Surely, there were more qualified people to whom the angel should appear. Yet, the angel spoke explicitly to them, and when the angel was joined by a company of countless other angels, there was no denying this was God's intention.

The Christmas story is full of surprises—so is God. Just wait until Jesus chooses disciples, eats with sinners, and forgives the worst among us. Just wait until he takes death and turns it into life.

That night began with shepherds. The angels brought good news for *all* people, including (and maybe especially) shepherds. It's one of God's great surprises, one worthy of a chorus of angels.

For reflection

* Why do you think the angel came to the shepherds?
* Why were shepherds uniquely qualified to hear the angels' song?
* Who are the shepherds today, and how can we follow their example?

Obedience

When the angels went away from them into heaven, the shepherds said to one another, "Let us go over to Bethlehem and see this thing that has happened, which the Lord has made known to us." —LUKE 2:15

"I guess we have no choice," the shepherds must have grumbled as they began the journey to Bethlehem. Still bewildered by the angels, they did as they were told. They were obedient, no matter how crazy it sounded.

I would love to have heard their conversation on the way to Bethlehem. I'm sure they worried they were being sent on a fool's errand. I'm sure they had second thoughts about the angels' words, but the shepherds continued, and, as a result, they were the first to see Jesus outside of Mary and Joseph. I imagine Joseph stood to protect Mary when they arrived, but I can see her hand reaching out to Joseph's arm as if to say, "It's okay. Let them join us."

In the creche of my childhood, there were two shepherds, one standing and the other kneeling. I placed them beside the sheep and looked on as the scene began to take shape. I wonder what was happening in the shepherds' minds as they entered the stable. How does seeing the infant feel? What made them stand in awe and kneel in reverence?

Sometimes, I have stood in awe and knelt in humility before God, but too often, I've been distracted by my own self-importance. I've been told where to go to find God and—unlike the shepherds—didn't follow the directions. The shepherds remind me it's never too late to follow where God leads. It might seem crazy at the time, but who knows, it might just lead me to a place where I see God.

For reflection

* What was it about the shepherds that made them obedient?
* When have you followed the voice of an angel, even if it seemed crazy?
* What do you think is harder, hearing or following God?

The Sheep

Keeping watch over their flock by night. —LUKE 2:8B

Then there were the sheep!

As I rearranged them at the shepherds' feet, I remember what a seminary professor once said: "Sheep are dumb! They only care about finding food, making other sheep, and staying with the rest of the flock." Once the laughter died down, he discussed how sheep wander aimlessly beside one another, with wool caked in dirt and who knows what. He explained that if one of the sheep went to the edge of a cliff and fell off, the others would follow. For emphasis, he repeated his opening line: "Sheep are dumb!"

As I looked at the sheep at the feet of the shepherds, I realized how similar we can be to sheep. We wander aimlessly beside one another, caked in the dirt of our own making, and will follow others even if they lead us off a cliff. Yes, like sheep, we can sometimes be quite dumb.

Yet, in the creche, the sheep reminded me how important shepherds are in keeping the sheep safe. Jesus would one day refer to himself as the "good shepherd." Maybe the nativity scene is a precursor to this vital lesson. Shepherds call and lead the sheep. One might even use a staff to redirect a wayward lamb. But shepherds also go searching for ones who get lost.

Seeing the sheep in the front row of the creche reminded me who we are and, more importantly, who that babe in the manger was—and is.

For reflection

* How are you, or others you know, like sheep?
* When have you followed the herd, even if it meant falling off a cliff?
* How do the shepherds remind us of who Jesus is?

The Angel

Then an angel of the Lord stood before them, and the glory of the Lord shone around them, and they were terrified. —LUKE 2:9

On the top of the stable was a hole into which I attached the angel. She (yes, I have always thought of the angel as a girl) was small with wings and a halo. She looked down from her place above the others as if to watch what she had foretold. She kept watch, giving witness to the miracle unfolding.

Placing her in her spot, I thought about this angel and all the angels God sends into our lives. Some speak to us; others sit beside us and watch our lives unfold. As a child, I wanted an angel to show up and talk to me like in the story, but I have since realized that I need to be careful what I wish for. When angels arrive, it's unsettling. No wonder their first words are usually, "Fear not!" Their presence is unsettling, even when they bring glad tidings. They remind us there's more to this world than what we see.

In the creche, the angel sat above the stable, watching over the birth of Christ. I believe they continue to watch over you and me. Our job is to look up, override our initial fears, and welcome their presence. Chances are, they'll bring good news for all people. It might be surprising or unsettling news, but I take comfort in the peace that exudes from the angel's face above the creche, with a smile that suggests, "Trust me."

For reflection

* Have you ever felt God's presence as if there was an angel beside you?
* Why do you think our initial reaction to God's presence is fear?
* How can you learn to quiet the world and your thoughts so that you can hear God's voice?

The Star

For we observed his star at its rising. —MATTHEW 2:2B

At the top of the creche was a place for the star. It was a big star, the kind that grabs your attention. Without the star, Bethlehem and the stable would have gone unnoticed. The star was there to offer direction but only to those wise enough to look up.

The star always made me feel jealous. The wise men got a star. They found Jesus because they had help. What about the rest of us? How do we, all these years later, find him too? "It's not fair," I remember whining to my parents. "How come we don't get a star?" After a poignant pause, my father smiled and said, "Who says we don't?"

I've thought about his response ever since. Yes, there was a star long ago, but God continues to send stars. They may not lead to a village in Palestine, but they do lead to Christ. Every time I hear someone's story, I see the many stars that have led them on their way. Some are events; others are people or conversations. These stars always bring light into darkness. They get a person's attention. They usually change a person's direction.

Seeing their stars helps me see some of my own. I've not always noticed, let alone followed, them, but I know they are there. The trick is looking up and following as best we can.

For reflection

* In what ways has God brought stars into your night skies?
* What is it about stars that are so important?
* How can you learn to recognize stars and follow them?

The Wise Men

Wise men from the East came to Jerusalem. —Matthew 2:1

They looked like kings, particularly in comparison to shepherds. Fancy robes and elaborate headwear gave them an air of importance. With reverence, I placed the wise men in the creche. "They were star gazers," someone once told me. "Men looking up into the sky trying to discern God's plan." I guess that was what made them wise.

The three figures in the creche reminded me that it isn't so much our abilities but our desires that lead us toward God. Sometimes, our abilities or what people think of us can get in the way of our spiritual journeys. Ultimately, who we are and who we follow matters more than what we do.

When I graduated from college, my uncle gave me a gift and a note. I have long forgotten the gift but not the note: "Congratulations on all your learning; now, may you be truly wise." He noted the difference between knowledge and wisdom, something I haven't always remembered. The three figures in the creche say it in a different way: it's not what you know but rather the one for whom you're searching.

Like them, hopefully, we'll be wise enough to look up and find what only our hearts can grasp.

For reflection

* In what ways have you come to know the difference between knowledge and wisdom?
* When has knowledge let you down, and when has wisdom surprised you?
* How could you look up this Christmas and find your way to God?

The Kings

Then Herod secretly called for the wise men and learned from them the exact time when the star had appeared. —MATTHEW 2:7

Although the gospel accounts refer to them as wise men, they have also been called "kings." There's even a hymn entitled "We Three Kings." In my school Christmas pageant, they were the ones with the fancy costumes and glittering props. I never got to be one. Because I could sing, I was always in the choir, sitting off to the side rather than under the spotlights on stage. The fancy robes, towering hats, and ornate boxes of gold, frankincense, and myrrh always made me envious. Their arrival was the climax of the show. They were the stars without delivering a line!

I now know I wanted to be special, stand out, and have a special role in the drama. Although my Christmas pageant days are over, my desire to be unique and to stand out remains, and it always gets in the way of my playing a meaningful role in the drama.

We live in a world that values kings (and queens). Jesus offers a sharp contrast to such a way of living. In fact, he teaches us to give up our colorful robes and expensive gifts and follow him.

As I placed the last king in place, I realized we all have roles in the drama, regardless of whether we are on stage or off to the side. We're all called to go to Bethlehem and see God for ourselves. What we do afterward is up to us. Hopefully, we'll be changed, as the kings were, and journey home by another way.

For reflection

* Were you ever in a Christmas pageant, and if so, what role did you play?
* What is your role in the Christian story today?
* Has your knowing Jesus led you home by another way?

Epiphany

When they saw that the star had stopped, they were overwhelmed with joy; On entering the house, they saw the child with Mary his mother; and they knelt down and paid him homage. —MATTHEW 2:10A

Epiphany is a fancy church term that means manifestation or seeing something for yourself. It's the name given to the moment when the wise men reached Bethlehem and saw Jesus for themselves. It's more than seeing with one's eyes. It's seeing with one's soul.

I'm sure the wise men talked about the Messiah on their long journey to Bethlehem. I imagine they shared what they thought he'd be like and how his arrival would change things, but nothing could have prepared them for the experience of seeing him for themselves. Wrapped in swaddling clothes and lying in a manger, he was unlike their most outlandish thoughts. The babe was like every other child they had seen, and yet, because they were wise, they saw in that babe more than what their eyes beheld. In him, they saw someone who would change the world forever. Seeing with the eyes of their souls made this an epiphany.

Like the wise men, we're on a long journey toward our hearts' deepest desire. With stars for guidance, we come to Bethlehem and see the child about whom we've heard so much. If we look with the eyes of our souls, we may well see much more than a baby in a manger 2,000 years ago. We'll see God-with-us, Emmanuel. When that happens, we'll see Jesus as if for the first time.

For reflection

* Can you recall a time when you saw something or someone as if for the first time?
* What changed? Was it something in them or in you?
* How could that experience help you have an epiphany of your own about Jesus?

The Gifts

Then, opening their treasure chests, they offered him gifts of gold, frankincense, and myrrh.—MATTHEW 2:11B

When I was little, I couldn't stop looking at the gifts the wise men brought into the stable. As someone who loved getting presents, I liked thinking about the gifts brought to Jesus. (Talk about how hard it is to give a gift to someone who has everything!) I must confess, I was let down when I heard what was in the three vessels: gold, frankincense, and myrrh. My father reminded me that it wasn't what they brought, but rather that they offered gifts. "It seems to me," he said, "that they're inviting us to follow their example." I asked, "What could I possibly give Jesus?"

It's a question I continue to ask.

Like the gifts carried by the wise men, gifts come in all kinds of boxes. They arrive in boxes—big and small, simple and fancy—but my wife taught me to not trust the box. Boxes can be deceiving. It's what's inside that matters. It's true of you and me and our God-given gifts. We all have gifts, and we're called to lay them at the feet of the child in the manger. The magic comes in watching what God does with our gifts.

Looking at the three gift-bearing wise men in the creche, I could hear the words from the familiar hymn: "What then can I give him, I will give my heart." That's enough. In fact, it's more than enough.

For reflection

- ✳ When were you touched by a gift you were given?
- ✳ What made it special?
- ✳ In what way can you offer Jesus a gift from your heart?

Shepherds and Kings

"What are *they* doing here?" one of the kings must have uttered, or maybe it was said by a shepherd. Either way, looking at the creche and seeing the shepherds and kings in the same scene, I couldn't help but wonder what was going on in their minds. We don't know if the shepherds were still there in Bethlehem when the wise men arrived, but seeing them together draws an important contrast.

It was the first—and not the last—time Jesus would bring unlikely people together. Throughout his life, he defied social groups. The figures in the creche reminded me of the poetic ways Jesus calls us to be one with our neighbors, whether they be shepherds or kings. Sometimes, in our desperation to belong, we push others aside and think of Jesus as a possession that belongs only to us or people like us.

But Jesus's birth was "good tidings of great joy for all people," not for *some* of us, but *all* of us. One of the most important lessons of Jesus is that he came into the world for shepherds *and* kings. When they are simply figures in a Christmas creche, it's an easy lesson to accept. When it's a lesson in our lives, it's much more difficult.

For reflection

* Do you consider yourself a shepherd or king/queen?
* How does that make you feel, and how does it influence how you see others?
* How has your faith brought you closer to others? How has it distanced you?

Joseph

When his mother had been engaged to Joseph. —MATTHEW 1:18B

The baby wasn't even his. Placing Joseph in his rightful place in the center of the creche, I couldn't help but think about his role in Jesus's life. Engaged to Mary, Joseph's life took an unexpected turn. It was too much for him to imagine, but an angel told him to have faith, which he did. I wonder how the story would differ if Joseph hadn't followed the angel's direction.

Older than Mary, he brought her safely to Bethlehem and did his best to make her comfortable in the stable. After Jesus was born, he led the family to safety in Egypt before returning to Nazareth. Joseph was no theologian or spiritual leader. He was a carpenter with a good and righteous heart. I imagine Joseph working with his son in the woodshop, teaching Jesus how to work with wood, smooth rough places, soften sharp edges, and work around knots. Although Jesus would not follow in Joseph's footsteps, what Joseph taught him about working with wood must have come in handy when he began working with people. When he met rough people or those with sharp edges or stubborn knots, he knew what to do... thanks to Joseph.

The gospels do not write much about Joseph, but his role was significant. As I placed him in the creche, I gave thanks for Joseph and all he taught Jesus.

For reflection

* Try to imagine a father-son moment between Jesus and Joseph. What are they doing? What are they talking about?
* If you were a piece of wood in God's hands, how would you hope to be transformed?
* How can you apply Joseph's lessons in carpentry to your life of faith?

Mary

Greetings, favored one! The Lord is with you. —LUKE 1:28

The figure of Mary, carved out of wood, didn't look like much. Kneeling, she looked smaller than Joseph. Her head was bowed, and her hands were folded. She looked meek, but I knew better. She was the one God chose above all others, and I have no doubt he chose her for a reason. She was the first in a long line of unlikely choices, but God knew what he was doing. She was chosen to bring God into the world, which was no small feat, but this seemingly demure figure was up to the task!

I've often wondered why God chose Mary. It wasn't because of her prestigious pedigree or her prominence in society. The only reason I can think of is she was someone God knew would have the grace, humility, and courage to say "yes." There were countless reasons to refuse the assignment and turn the angel down, but Mary trusted God's plan. She had faith in God despite the outlandishness of what she was asked to do.

As I stood back and looked at Mary beside the manger, I felt her invitation to follow her example. Although we may not be asked to bear a child, I believe we are asked to bring Christ into the world. It's never easy work, but it's crucial. Regardless of how we bring Christ into the world and follow Mary's example, it all begins with saying "yes."

Who knows? We might end up bringing God into the world in some unique, unexpected way.

For reflection

* What do you admire most about Mary?
* What do you think made her reluctant to say yes?
* Why do you think she said yes in the end? How can you learn to say yes, too?

The Manger

And she gave birth to her firstborn son and wrapped him in bands of cloth, and laid him in a manger, because there was no place for them in the inn. —LUKE 2:7

The manger was the smallest piece of the creche so far. It was not much more than a box with legs, but its purpose caused me to put the manger in its place with reverence. When I was young, I painted it gold, but only fragments of that paint remain. I wanted to make this vital part of the nativity stand out, but looking at the chipped paint, I wonder if the manger didn't want such attention. Maybe its power was in its simplicity, its ordinariness. It was just a feeding trough being used for a different purpose. Perhaps it was called to serve another kind of food.

Many of us are hungry for God, and some might say we're starving for God. In a world that offers so many other things to "eat," the manger stands in sharp contrast. What (or who) it offers is far from what we want, yet it provides all we need.

Like the animals, our hunger leads us to the manger. Despite its small size, there's room for everyone. It's time to return, to take our places again, and to receive the food for which we hunger.

For reflection

* For what are you most hungry?
* In what ways have you satisfied your hunger with the wrong food?
* How can you come to the manger, make room for others, and eat the meal you most need?

64

Waiting

The worst part of Christmas is the waiting! Just ask children who see presents waiting under the tree or reach up to hang their empty stocking by the fireplace. "Can't we just *pretend* it's Christmas?" I remember asking my parents, knowing their answer already.

Waiting is not something the world tells us we should have to do. Everywhere you look, you can see a new way of getting something faster and more efficiently, yet waiting is one of the great spiritual practices. Waiting reminds us that we are not in charge; we cannot make certain things happen. When it comes to God coming into the world and into our lives, we must accept God's timing, which means we must learn how to wait.

Christmas is not something we do. It's what God does.

"The Word became flesh and dwelt among us," the Bible says. "You shall call him, Emmanuel, which means God-with-us," it also says. This time of year allows us to hear those words anew, to hold that hope in our hearts as if for the first time. We may open the box, unwrap the figures, and put them in place, but, in the end, it is God who comes and is with us, God who becomes flesh.

All we can do is wait, but that's more than enough.

For reflection

* Are you good at waiting?
* Why is waiting such an important spiritual practice?
* How can your ability to wait increase your connection to God?

Christ

And suddenly there was with the angel a multitude of the heavenly host, praising God and saying, "Glory to God in the highest, and on earth peace among those with whom God favors!"—LUKE 2:13-14

I couldn't find him. After unwrapping each item of the creche and putting them in place, I realized I was missing the most important piece of all: Jesus! I looked in the box again. I unwrapped every piece of newspaper, but the baby was nowhere to be found. It wasn't until I lifted the box and shook it that I heard a sound. Something rattled, and I looked again. There in the corner was the small wooden baby. His arms were opened wide, just like I remembered. It was as if he was saying, "Pick me up," or maybe he was saying, "Let me pick *you* up." Either way, I reached down and took this final piece to its rightful place. All the other pieces were waiting. The creche had looked complete, but then I realized the scene wasn't truly complete until the baby was in his proper place.

How like our lives that moment was, I thought. We strive to arrange all the people and places and things to create a scene that looks complete—but isn't. Something or someone is missing, and nothing makes sense until we have Christ at the center. We might need to search for the missing piece; we might need to open the box and look again. Then, when we least expect it, we hear or see something, and our hearts leap.

This is the one for whom we have been searching.

This is the one who has been missing.

This is the one who makes our lives complete.

For reflection

* When have you searched for Jesus?
* In what way(s) did you find him in an unlikely place or ordinary wrapping?
* How can you place him in the center and make your life complete?

Chip Bristol

After a career serving Episcopal schools as chaplain and Head of School, Chip Bristol has turned his attention to writing spiritual books as well as a weekly blog. Filled with Chip's energy and creativity, this book seeks to bring new life to the familiar Christmas story. He and his wife, Louise, live in Greensboro, North Carolina, and have a blended family scattered all over the country. Visit his website: www.withoutacollar.com.

Kelly Rightsell

Following years as an art educator and entrepreneur, Kelly Rightsell enjoys painting, sculpting, and creating every day. The rich variety and vibrant colors speak to all who know her work. Kelly and her husband, Brian, live in Greensboro, North Carolina, and have three grown and flown children. Visit her website: www.kellyrightsell.com.

But the angel said to them, "Do not be afraid; for see—I am bringing you good news of great joy for all the people: to you is born this day in the city of David a Savior, who is the Messiah, the Lord. This will be a sign for you: you will find a child wrapped in bands of cloth and lying in a manger." —LUKE 2:10-12

Made in the USA
Columbia, SC
16 December 2024

5f73d848-6d98-4d42-a408-898b2a67817eR01